Jane Austen in Bath

Also published by the Jane Austen Society

Fanny Knight's Diaries: Jane Austen through her niece's eyes
by Deirdre Le Faye

Godmersham Park, Kent – before, during, and since Jane Austen's day
by Nigel Nicolson

Jane Austen's family and Tonbridge
by Margaret Wilson

My Aunt Jane Austen: a memoir
by Caroline Austen

Reminiscences of Caroline Austen
ed. by Deirdre Le Faye

Collected Reports 1949-1965; 1966-1975; 1976-1985; 1986-1995

In association with Carcanet Press:
Collected Poems and verse of the Austen family
ed. David Selwyn

Jane Austen: A Celebration
ed. Maggie Lane and David Selwyn

Jane Austen
in Bath

JEAN FREEMAN

Revised Edition

THE JANE AUSTEN SOCIETY

First published in Great Britain in 1969

Revised edition first published in 2002
by the Jane Austen Society
c/o Jane Austen's House, Chawton, Alton, Hampshire GU34 1SD

ISBN 0-9538174-1-5

Printed by Sarsen Press, 22 Hyde Street, Winchester SO23 7DR

Preface

Jane Austen in Bath was written by Jean Freeman in 1969 at the request of The Jane Austen Society whose Honorary Secretary at that time, Sir Hugh Smiley, greatly encouraged Jean in this project. Since that time, more information about Jane Austen and about Bath has become available and at the Society's request, and with the approval of Jean Freeman, this revised and updated version of Jean's book has been prepared by Gavin Turner, in consultation with Deirdre Le Faye.

Thanks are due to Michael Davis for taking so many of the photographs and to the Bath Tourism Office for allowing the reproduction of the map, and of the photographs appearing on pages 11, 12 and 24.

The quotations from *Jane Austen's Letters* are taken, with kind permission, from Deirdre Le Faye's 1995 edition (Oxford University Press).

The Jane Austen Society gratefully acknowledges a financial contributions from the Jane Austen Bath and Bristol group towards production costs.

The Jane Austen Society
August 2002

I

No admirer of Jane Austen and her works should be without some knowledge of the City of Bath and of the considerable part that it played in her life – this despite the fact that it was by no means a favourite place of hers, and that she so much preferred country life to that of the town.

Jane's acquaintance with Bath began in her early twenties and continued until her thirtieth year. During the latter part of that time she lived there for five years with her parents and her sister, Cassandra. At the time of her earliest visits Bath was still enjoying that popularity which had been at its height in the middle of the 18th century when, in the eyes of the beau monde, it was surpassed in importance only by London itself. When Jane's father retired there in 1801, however, Bath's place as a centre for fashionable visitors was gradually being taken by the ever-growing number of seaside resorts, of which Brighton was the most famous. It was then becoming more a place of residence for retired people, such as lawyers, clergymen and other members of the professional classes. Bath's brilliant heyday gave place at the turn of the century to a kind of Indian summer. The fashionable visitors might have departed but all the advantages, natural and acquired, which had made Bath one of England's foremost cities, remained; the Baths themselves, the General Hospital and all the medical facilities, the Assembly Rooms, the Theatre, circulating libraries and excellent shops. It was also, with its fine streets, squares and crescents, a model of eighteenth-century planning and architectural elegance which has never been equalled anywhere else in this country.

As such Bath would obviously have been well known to the reading public of Jane Austen's day and that she herself took this completely for granted is very evident. It was perfectly natural for her to think of Bath as the place where one might attend balls or card parties, visit the theatre, or go for a cure; for after all, though Jane never really liked Bath, it had provided her with her only real experience of city life, apart from various visits to London.

So it is that references to Bath occur from time to time throughout all Jane Austen's novels. In *Emma* it is to Bath that Mr Elton goes to seek a wife. In *Pride and Prejudice* we hear at the end that Wickham is allowed to go to Bath to enjoy himself when Lydia visits Pemberley. In *Mansfield Park* Mr Crawford's sudden departure is accounted for by his having an engagement 'to meet his Uncle in Bath'. The Reverend Dr Grant goes to Bath, without doubt for a cure, and in *Sense and Sensibility*, when the Palmers are obliged to leave their house because of Marianne's illness, they take refuge with friends 'on the other side of Bath'. In the lesser known *Lady Susan* part of the plot hinges on Mr Johnson's being removed to Bath, where, as his wife writes to Lady Susan: 'If the waters are favourable to his constitution and my wishes, he will be laid up with the gout many weeks'. These are some of the occasions when Bath is mentioned and there are many others. Yet in addition to mere references to Bath, Jane Austen also made it the main setting for two of her six novels, which fact alone would make some study of the city by her admirers worth while. In the one, *Northanger Abbey*, completed in 1803, she describes the gaieties of a Bath she herself had known as a young lady. In the other, *Persuasion,* written thirteen years afterwards, she writes about the more sober Bath which she knew in her later years.

Our main source of information about the time that Jane Austen and members of her family spent in Bath is the letters that she herself wrote, nearly always to her sister Cassandra. We learn only indirectly from them about Bath itself, as she was writing to someone who obviously knew the place as well as she did. It seems appropriate, therefore, at this point to give a brief history and some description of this city.

Bath is in Somerset about a hundred miles west of London, on the Bristol Avon. It owes its existence primarily to its hot springs; legend has it that the British prince Bladud, in pre-Roman days, was cured of leprosy by bathing in the healing waters. The Romans built a city there, Aquae Sulis, with magnificent baths and a temple dedicated to the goddess Sul Minerva.

After the Roman period the city fell into decay; the baths silted up and lay buried but preserved until excavated in the 1880s. Thus the Roman Baths were unknown to Jane Austen and her contemporaries, but there were other baths in the city.

The Saxons built their own town and church on the ruins of the Roman city. Later came the Normans, but the large church which they built on the same site was destroyed by fire in 1137 and the Abbey which Jane Austen knew and which exists today, though with extensive additions and restorations, dates from the end of the 15th century.

Through the Middle Ages the healing powers of the hot springs continued to be well known and other baths were built. In the 16th century Bath was granted a charter by Queen Elizabeth I and expanded to include Barton Fields in the west and to the east the parish of Walcot. Thenceforward royal visits to Bath continued regularly and its success as a health and pleasure resort was assured. Fashionable visitors came in even larger number following Queen Anne's two visits at the beginning of the 18th century.

From this period onwards Bath always had a Master of Ceremonies in charge of its entertainment and hospitality, a custom continued until the First World War. Most famous of these was Richard ('Beau') Nash, often called the uncrowned 'King of Bath', so great was his success in this role during the first fifty years of the 18th century. During his 'reign' the streets were properly paved, lighted and cleaned, lodging houses were improved and music and well regulated entertainment provided.

One has only to study the many plaques on the houses of Bath today to realise that few at that time who were famous in society, politics or letters, failed to reside there at some period of their lives. At the same time behind the glittering façade, the treatment of those who sought the benefit of the healing waters went on and the city was justly famous for its excellent doctors, one of whom, Dr William Oliver, founded with others the Bath General Hospital (now the Royal Mineral Water Hospital), which opened to admit patients in 1742.

While Beau Nash was improving the social amenities, Bath itself was being transformed and greatly enlarged on the southern slopes of Lansdown

Hill above the old town: later it stretched across the river into the new district of Bathwick. Conceived as a practical scheme to provide elegant accommodation for the ever increasing number of fashionable visitors, the extensions amounted to what was virtually a new city. These were carried out in the 'Palladian' style (after the Italian, Andrea Palladio who lived from 1518-80), which was essentially a rendering in English material of the Roman architectural tradition. Those responsible were local builders and architects, most famous of whom were the Woods, father and son, under the patronage of Ralph Allen, one time postal clerk, who had settled in Bath and made a fortune by reorganising the country's postal services and later by developing local stone quarries.

Perhaps John Wood the elder's main contribution was the impressive Queen Square, finished in 1735 and lying outside the original northern city boundary. From here Gay Street rises steeply to the Circus, which was finished for him by his son in the 1760s. This, as its name suggests, is a complete circle of houses designed with three tiers of columns of the three classical orders, Doric, Ionic and Corinthian, supporting a continuous frieze. It was joined by Brock Street to the younger Wood's greatest masterpiece, the Royal Crescent, finished in 1775 and consisting of thirty houses with 114 great Ionic columns supporting a continuous cornice, in the form of a semi-ellipse over 600 feet long. This magnificent crescent and the Circus, built as all Bath buildings of the golden oolite stone from nearby quarries, were always designed to accommodate the wealthier visitors; the Austens never considered either place when looking for somewhere to live in Bath. For those with more modest incomes the younger Wood and his successors built the surrounding streets, later reaching up steep Lansdown Hill to Camden and Lansdown Crescents, with their wonderful views of the surrounding countryside; then eastwards through the Paragon and the Vineyards to Walcot Church, all finished towards the end of the eighteenth century. By this time society had moved to these areas, away from the old city. In 1771 the two lower sets of Rooms, beside the river, and dating from the earlier part of the century, were joined by the Assembly Rooms (known in Jane's day as the Upper Rooms) built by the younger Wood next to the

The Royal Crescent

Pulteney Bridge

Circus. These became, and remain today, one of the major glories of Bath; for although gutted during the air raids of 1942, they have been faithfully rebuilt and restored to their original splendour and can be seen today virtually as Jane Austen knew them.

In 1774 Pulteney Bridge, Robert Adam's only work in Bath, was opened. In Florentine style, with shops lining the carriageway across it, it connected Bath with the then new district of Bathwick. Unfortunately the ambitious plans to develop this area were never completed, owing to lack of funds, but the elegant and spacious Pulteney Street was finished, together with several smaller streets leading out of it, and the one-time Sydney Hotel (now the Holburne Museum of Art) at its far end. Next to this were the famous Sydney Gardens, Bath's equivalent of London's Vauxhall Gardens, and it was here in Sydney Place overlooking these gardens, that the Austens, after much anxious searching, decided to live when they finally settled in Bath.

In the 1790s Thomas Baldwin, the architect responsible for Pulteney Street, rebuilt the Pump Room beside the Abbey in place of the earlier buildings of 1706. With its classic interior of great Corinthian three-quarter columns this magnificent room was devoted to the daily meeting and water drinking of Bath's many visitors, which function it still performs.

Bath was renowned as a shopping centre and many were the commissions that Jane Austen undertook for friends and members of her family whenever she was there. Milsom Street was perhaps the most famous, as it is today. Built originally in the 1760s for residential purposes, by Jane's day it had become also a centre for shops and banks. Here too is the beautiful little Octagon Chapel, built in 1767 and up to fairly recent times used as a hall for social and other gatherings. It was a proprietary or subscription chapel, of which Bath had at least half a dozen, and was advertised as containing 'recesses, fireplaces, carpeted floors, and every accommodation of ease and refinement of luxury'.[1] There are quite a number of references to chapels in Jane's letters from Bath and the Austens appear to have attended several of them at one time or another.

Bath's theatre was opened in 1750 in Orchard Street, not far from the Abbey. It was the first theatre outside London protected by a Royal Patent

– granted in 1768 – when it became known as the Theatre Royal, Bath. Here Sarah Siddons, the Kembles and other famous players performed and this was the theatre that Jane knew best, for the present Theatre Royal in Beauford Square was not opened until the summer of 1805. The old theatre has now become the Masonic Hall.

Not surprisingly Bath offered its visitors a high standard of accommodation. As one visitor in the early 19th century wrote : 'Lodgings are not only very numerous, but are distinguished for the elegance, convenience, and comfort, which they afford the visitors. In the course of a walk of five or ten minutes about the City, after the arrival of a family, suitable apartments may be procured, with the utmost ease'.[2]

Besides the many lodging houses there were at least a dozen excellent inns and of these the White Hart, opposite Abbey Churchyard, long since demolished, was the most famous. Many of these had extensive stabling and were engaged in the coaching and posting business, in which respect Bath was particularly well served. There was a regular coach service to London, three times a week, taking two days, and in the summer 'flying coaches' took only half that time. For the less wealthy and for all types of merchandise there were wagons which could make the journey in three days. Numerous other vehicles journeyed to such places as Bristol, Exeter, Salisbury, Frome, Devizes and Chippenham.

The widespread system of cross posts, set up by Ralph Allen in the middle of the 18th century and stretching across the country, included his own city and in 1784 John Palmer, a native of Bath, started his mail coach services to London. Leaving Bath in the evening at 5.30 p.m. these coaches reached the City of London by 8 a.m. the next morning. So successful was this that similar services to other places soon followed.

This, then, gives some idea of the Bath that Jane Austen knew. In many ways it is remarkably unchanged today, in spite of considerable demolition of old buildings in the city and the appearance of many new houses on the outskirts. We may now consider those parts of Bath with which she was most closely associated.

II

The Austen family's connection with Bath began a good many years before Jane was born. Her maternal grandmother, Mrs Thomas Leigh, daughter of Dr John Walker and grand-daughter of James Perrot of Northleigh, Oxfordshire, lived in Bath as a widow, her husband having died in 1764, after his retirement there. In Bath also their younger daughter Cassandra (Jane's mother) had been married to the Reverend George Austen, rector of Steventon in Hampshire in April 1764. The elder daughter Jane married the Reverend Edward Cooper, who was rector of Whaddon near Bath in the early 1780s. Their only brother James succeeded in 1751, when he was fifteen years old, to the Northleigh estate on the death of his great-uncle, Thomas Perrot, and assumed the name Leigh Perrot. He married Jane Cholmeley in 1764 and lived in Bath although he had a country home, Scarlets, near Maidenhead in Berkshire, about thirty miles out of London on the Bath road.

In 1768 Mrs Austen's mother died but the close association between the two sisters and their brother continued. James, having been a regular visitor to Bath for some years to seek relief from frequent attacks of gout, finally took a house there at No. 1 Paragon, where later his younger sister and her family often stayed. Letters to and from Bath must have been a regular feature of the Steventon children's childhood. The girls, Cassandra and Jane, knew well their Cooper cousins, Jane and Edward. Jane Cooper had been their companion in their early schooldays at Oxford and Southampton and later at the Abbey House School at Reading. In 1783 Mrs Cooper died, from the same 'putrid fever' (typhus), as that from which the girls had suffered in Southampton, and in 1784, her husband left Whaddon for Sonning, Berkshire, where he was vicar until his death in 1792. He and his wife are both buried in Whaddon church. The Leigh Perrots were childless and they always welcomed the Austen family to their home in the Paragon, although we have no actual record of any visits to Bath before November 1797 when Jane was twenty-two. We hear for the first time of a visit to Bath in that year from Jane herself in a letter to Cassandra of 17 May 1799. Written from 13 Queen Square, where she is in lodgings with her brother Edward and some of his family, she makes a brief reference to a previous stay. Telling of the dismal journey they have just had from Devizes, she says: 'it has rained almost all the way & our first veiw (*sic*) of Bath has been just as gloomy as it was last November twelvemonth'. Of this earlier visit we know nothing more, but it is most probable that Jane stayed with the Leigh Perrots at No. 1 The Paragon, and it is here that we should first think of her in Bath.

To get to Bath from Steventon the Austens travelled by coach via Andover and Devizes and then down over Kingsdown Hill to join the London to Bath road about three miles east of the city. It was a familiar journey for them, and approaching Bath from that direction today we know that we are looking at almost exactly the same scene as would have greeted the eyes of the Steventon family at the end of their long journey, so little has it altered. The silhouette of Lansdown Hill, running steeply down into the town with its Abbey tower, church spires and many chimney pots – this was the scene to which Jane was referring, when she wrote to Cassandra one late afternoon in May 1801, immediately after arriving at her uncle's house in the Paragon. As so often, she was teasing a little and in any case was usually rather critical of Bath, so she says: 'The first veiw of Bath in fine weather does not answer my expectations; I think I see more distinctly thro' Rain. —The Sun was got behind everything, and the appearance of the place from the top of Kingsdown, was all vapour, shadow, smoke & confusion'.

Leaving Kingsdown and entering the outskirts of Bath through Lambridge the Austens would at last have reached their destination, the Paragon, here forming the end of the London Road as it finally enters the city. A gently curving terrace of twenty-one houses, it was one of a number of such streets, stretching up from the old city, built towards the end of the eighteenth century. Then, as now, a large part of the traffic from London

No. 1 The Paragon

St Swithin's, Walcot

to Bath and the West Country passed along it. A few yards beyond the Paragon, York House, still a well known hotel, was once a terminus for coaches going to and from London and other parts. The Austens would have had to travel the length of the Paragon, alongside the wide raised pavement, to reach Mr Leigh Perrot's house at the extreme southern end. The raising of the pavement above the road is a not uncommon sight in Bath, where the 18th-century planners anticipated by two hundred years the 'modern' idea of separating pedestrians, where possible, from the dirt and danger of busy streets.

Outwardly unchanged, though today divided into flats like so many of Bath's houses, No. 1 is a fairly large house of four storeys (and basement), with a rather gloomy view looking on to the street in the front but with fine views across the city at the back. In common with a large number of other Georgian houses in Bath, the windows of No. 1 today no longer have their glazing bars and small square glass panes but instead are of plain plate glass. The stonework here is somewhat darkened by years of damp and grime but in Jane Austen's day it would still have been the pale golden colour typical of Bath stone when new and which must have made Georgian Bath so very attractive to look at, although Jane could once, through Anne Elliot, speak of 'the white glare of Bath'.

At the northern end of the Paragon, farthest from the Leigh Perrots' house, stands the Georgian Church of St Swithin, Walcot parish church. Little is known of the original building but there was a church on this site from at least the year 1000. It is of particular interest to Jane Austen's admirers, for it was in the old Walcot Church that her parents were married in 1764. The entry can still be seen in the marriage register, where it reads:

'George Austen Batchelor of the Parish of Steventon in the County of Hants and Cassandra Leigh Spinster of this Parish were Married in this Church by License this Twenty sixth Day of April in the Year One Thousand Seven Hundred and Sixty four by me Thos Powys Minister.'

The witnesses were James Leigh Perrot and Jane Leigh.

On 24 January of that same year there is also an entry in the Parish register recording the death of Mrs Austen's father, the Reverend Thomas Leigh.

In the 1770s, this old church was pulled down and the present one – in the neo-classical style – built on the foundations, which can still be seen forming the walls of the crypt. It was enlarged in 1788 and the charming spire added in 1790. The interior is light and pleasing with a wooden gallery on three sides and remains very much as Jane Austen knew it. Jane frequently speaks in her letters to Cassandra of having been to church but never mentions Walcot Church by name. Nevertheless we can be certain that it was well known to all the Austen family and, in view of their connections with it, we know it must have had a special place in their affections. Here Mr Austen was buried when he died in Bath in 1805. His grave is in the crypt; and the ledgerstone which covered it, having been removed in the 1960s, was mounted in the year 2000 in the garden beside the church, accompanied by a plaque explaining the Austen connections with Bath. Both are now clearly visible through the railings which surround the garden ground. On the ledgerstone is inscribed very simply:

'Under this stone rest the remains of the Revd George Austen, Rector of Steventon and Dean in Hampshire—who departed this life the 21st January, 1805, Aged 73 years'.

It is interesting to note that Madame d'Arblay, otherwise Fanny Burney, the novelist whose books Jane Austen knew and admired and who lived in Bath for a time and died there in 1840, is also buried at Walcot. Interesting too, to Jane Austen's admirers, is that the older guide books of Bath told of Fanny Burney's connection with the city but never even mentioned Jane Austen, an omission which has now been rectified.

The Paragon, at the upper end of the town, was reasonably well placed for visiting the nearby shops, drinking the waters at the Pump Room or for dancing or going to concerts at the Assembly Rooms and we can be sure that members of the Austen family entered into all these activities whenever they stayed there. Nevertheless, for our first full account of a visit by Jane Austen to Bath we must leave the Paragon and consider Queen Square close by; for here Jane stayed at No. 13 for over five weeks in 1799 and we can learn a great deal about that visit from the letters which she wrote to Cassandra whilst there.

For some months Jane's brother Edward had been in poor health and was advised to try a cure at Bath. He journeyed up from Kent with his wife Elizabeth and their two elder children and two servants, and invited Jane and her mother to join them in the lodgings he had taken at No. 13 Queen Square. The whole party travelled together to Bath and reached there at one o'clock from Devizes, where they had stayed overnight. Almost at once Jane sat down in the drawing-room at Queen Square to write to Cassandra, for she had little or no unpacking to do as her trunk was to come on by wagon from Devizes, having proved too heavy for the coach.

Jane's first letter from Bath in 1799 is headed 'No.13 —Queen's Square —Friday May 17th', and begins with an account of their successful journey and excellent dinner and rooms they had had at Devizes. She regrets only that rain during the last part of the journey had spoiled her sister-in-law Elizabeth's first view of Bath, which she, alone of the grown ups, had never visited before. The rain had also meant that it was too wet and dirty for them to alight at the Paragon when they stopped there on their way in and enquired after Mr Leigh Perrot's health.

The lodgings were all that they had hoped for. Their landlady, a Mrs Bromley, was 'a fat woman in mourning', with a little black kitten running about the house. The stairs were such that Mrs Austen was able easily to mount the double flight to the second floor, where she and Jane had their two rooms, leaving Elizabeth with the first-floor room, leading off the drawing-room. All the rooms were pleasant and comfortable, Jane's 'quite as large as our bedroom at home, & my Mother's is not materially less' with the beds 'both as large as any at Steventon; & I have a very nice chest of Drawers & a Closet full of shelves'.

They were none of them any the worse for their journey and, though Edward seemed a little tired, Jane was hoping that 'the bustle of sending for Tea, Coffee & Sugar &c., and going out to taste a cheese himself will do him good'. The rain had ceased and the pavements were 'getting very white again', as Bath's granite-squared pavements always do shortly after even the heaviest downpour. They had seen a long list of visitors in the newspapers so would not lack for company during their stay, and there was also 'a public Breakfast in Sydney Gardens every morning, so that we shall not be wholly starved'.

Finally, looking up from her letter, she says: 'the prospect from the Drawingroom window at which I now write, is rather picturesque, as it commands a perspective veiw of the left side of Brock Street, broken by three Lombardy Poplars in the Garden of the last house in Queen's Parade'. Altogether Jane liked their situation which she found far more cheerful than the Paragon and concluded by sending a 'great deal of Love from everybody'.

This first letter from Jane would have told Cassandra all those things that she wanted to know, particularly such domestic details as the number and size and furnishings of their rooms. There was no need to say anything about the Square itself, already well known to Cassandra, but those who do not know Bath might like some further description of it. No. 13 is on the south side of Queen Square, on the corner at the western end. Another typical Georgian town house of four storeys (and basement), it is today let out as offices, but outwardly it looks much as it must have done to the Austens in 1799, though here again the stonework is somewhat darkened by damp and age.

Queen Square was completed by John Wood the elder in 1735. Originally he had intended to treat all four sides of it in the same manner but in the end it was the north side, facing into the sun, that he made the most magnificent. The southern and eastern sides are plain and simple, though with some handsome doorways, and the western side has two fine houses, originally detached and then later joined to complete that side of the Square by what is now the home of the Bath Royal Literary and Scientific Institution. The whole north end of Queen Square, though a terrace of houses, appears as a single façade, a Palladian gem with central Corinthian pillars, surmounted by a plain pediment, producing an effect full of grandeur. Had Jane looked a little further to the right out of the drawing-room window of No. 13, she would have seen this and also the Square's garden in the foreground, with its central obelisk erected by Beau Nash to commemorate the visit of Frederick, Prince of Wales in 1738.

No. 13 Queen Square, with Beechen Cliff in the distance

The Pump Room

There are three further letters (2, 11 and 19 June) written by Jane to Cassandra during this particular visit but in these, too, she confines herself to writing only what is of particular and personal interest to her sister. Thus, though she writes on 2 June that Edward's health is improving and he 'drinks at the Hetling Pump, is to bathe tomorrow, & try Electricity on Tuesday,' she does not say that the Hetling Pump House, opened in the early 1770s, was opposite the Hot Bath in a road which is now called Hot Bath Street. Nor does she describe the Bath where he bathed, or mention the fact that he would have been carried there and back by sedan chair, as accommodation for undressing and dressing was so limited. We do not learn if Edward ever 'went to drink the waters' and listen to the music in the fashionable Pump Room, or joined the promenaders strolling on the parades by the river or around the Orange Grove near by (called after the Prince of Orange) or if he attended daily service in the Abbey; all these were favourite occupations for fashionable invalids and their friends.

Instead there is much talk of numerous purchases for Jane herself and her relations, taking advantage of Bath's excellent shops. But again though we hear much of bonnets and trimmings, shoes and stockings, cloaks and laces, we hear nothing of the shops themselves or even a mention of that famous shopping thoroughfare, Milsom Street. However, a description of it by an early 19th-century visitor enables us to visualise the scene: 'All is bustle and gaiety: numerous dashing equipages passing and repassing, others gracing the doors of the tradesmen; sprinkled here and there with the invalids in the comfortable sedans and easy two-wheeled carriages, all anxious to participate in this active part of Bath, giving a sort of finish to the scene. The shops are tastefully laid out; capacious and elegant;... In short Milsom and Bond Streets afford to the utmost extent every thing towards supplying the real or imaginary wants of the visitors: containing libraries to improve the mind —musical repositories to enrich their taste and science —confectioners to invite the most fastidious appetite —tailors, milliners, &c. of the highest eminence in the fashionable world.'[3]

Bath is still famous for its shops, though none now remain that Jane Austen would have known. When, however, she speaks in a later letter (3

January 1801) of 'disordering' her stomach 'with Bath bunns', present-day visitors to Bath will know that these buns are still made and are as popular now as then.

In Jane's letter to Cassandra from Queen Square, of 2 June 1799, the magnificent and famous Royal Crescent is referred to only as the place where 'Lady Willoughby is to present the Colours to some Corps of Yeomanry or other', which ceremony she and her sister-in-law hoped to attend. The Crescent itself, with its wide pavement, broad cobbled carriageway and with a lawn in front enclosed in iron railings, was always a popular place for visitors to walk, particularly on Sundays. In front of it used to be the Crescent Fields, another favourite spot for walks and where such displays as Jane mentions often took place. Today it is a park, Victoria Park, opened in 1830 by Princess Victoria, and equally popular with Bath's many visitors.

From this same letter we also learn that Jane and Elizabeth were hoping to attend an open-air concert with illuminations and fireworks in Sydney Gardens. Jane wrote that she looked forward to this evening concert with pleasure 'as the Gardens are large enough for me to get pretty well beyond the reach of its sound'. Heavy rain spoiled this occasion but they went again a fortnight later, arriving at nine p.m., after the music was over, and 'then were in very good time for the Fire-works, which were really beautiful'.

In Jane's letter of 19 June, she tells of the quiet routine in Queen Square, broken only by a dinner with a Mr Evelyn, a friend of her brother, who had a house in adjoining Queen's Parade as well as one in Kent, and by tea-drinking in 'the Paragon with my uncle'.

Earlier, she had described two country walks which she had enjoyed.[4] The first on a Friday evening with friends, the Mapletons, when she tells Cassandra, who probably did not know this particular walk: 'We took a very charming walk from 6 to 8 up Beacon Hill, & across some fields to the Village of Charlecombe, which is sweetly situated in a little green Valley, as a Village with such a name ought to be'. The second was when we 'walked to Weston one evening last week, & liked it very much'. This little village, now joined to Bath and much enlarged by several new housing estates, lies about two miles due west of Bath and it is still possible to take Jane's probable route over Sion Hill and using part of the Cotswold Way to reach it.

Jane once referred to herself as 'a desperate walker'[5] and anyone today who cares to undertake the various walks in and around Bath enjoyed by Jane, her friends and her heroines, will no doubt be astonished at the activity displayed by these supposedly frail ladies of two hundred years ago. The excellent knowledge of the environs of Bath that Jane acquired through these long walks she attributed also to Eleanor and Henry Tilney in *Northanger Abbey*.

She herself no doubt explored the woodland ways around Bathwick Hill, walked over Claverton Down, where Ralph Allen had his Sham Castle built to improve the view from his town house, and walked along the Avon Valley to the little village of Claverton; one can still do all this today. She must have known every step of the way taken by Catherine Morland and the Tilneys to Beechen Cliff, 'that noble hill, whose beautiful verdure and hanging coppice render it so striking an object from almost every opening in Bath'.[6]

The hills of Bath, though helping to give it its unique charm, are very steep indeed; yet Mrs Austen, by then in her sixties, when lodging in Gay Street in 1805, walked up to Lansdown Crescent to see a friend one Sunday after chapel and another time Jane mentions a walk out to the then detached village of Twerton, about two miles south west of Bath. Catherine Morland, in *Northanger Abbey* walks frequently between her own lodgings in Pulteney Street and those of her friends, the Thorpes, in Edgar Buildings. A sudden shower of rain, not the steepness of the hill, is responsible for Miss Elliot's seeking a lift in Lady Dalrymple's carriage from Milsom Street to Camden Place (now Camden Crescent) named after Lord Camden, one-time Recorder of Bath. Anne Elliot walks down and back from Camden Place to Westgate Buildings quite alone, to visit poor Mrs Smith; finally, when she has called on foot at the White Hart, near the Abbey, to see the Musgrove family, she is still able to make the journey home on Captain Wentworth's arm and, 'as they slowly paced the gradual ascent', was quite equal to indulging 'in those explanations of what had directly preceded the present moment, which were so poignant and so ceaseless in interest'.[7]

Jane's final letter from Queen Square, 19 June 1799, tells Cassandra that: 'The play on Saturday is I hope to conclude our Gaieties here'. Something that Jane did not mention was the name of the play or plays that she was hoping to see. The *Bath Herald and Register* for Saturday, 29 June, 1799, contains the following information on the Bath theatre given by a correspondent: 'The pleasing spectacle of Blue Beard, after a short interval in consequence of the spring benefits, was again brought forward Saturday evening last with undiminished attraction. The Romance of Blue Beard was preceded by Kotzebue's admirable drama of "The Birth-day". If the German author has justly drawn down censure for the immorality of his productions for the stage, this may be accepted as his *amende honourable*— it is certainly throughout unexceptionable, calculated to promote the best interest of virtue, and the purest principles of benevolence; and though written much in the style of Sterne, it possesses humour without a single broad Shandyism.'

It was another of Kotzebue's plays, *Natural Son* published in England as *Lovers' Vows*, which Jane Austen used in *Mansfield Park* (in a translation by Mrs Inchbald, somewhat toned down to suit English audiences) and which caused such a storm when Sir Thomas Bertram returned unexpectedly from the West Indies to find his family rehearsing it.

III

About two months after Jane and her mother and brother had left Bath an event occurred there, involving her maternal uncle and aunt, the Leigh Perrots, which must have been the cause of a great deal of anxiety for the whole Austen family.

On the morning of 8 August 1799 this highly respected couple set out from their home in the Paragon and walked down to Stall Street. Here at a haberdasher's shop on the corner of Bath Street, known as 'Smith's', and kept by the late owner's sister, a Miss Elizabeth Gregory, Mrs Leigh Perrot bought and paid for a length of black lace. She left, carrying her parcel, but a little later, as she and her husband walked back again past Smith's, out came Miss Gregory and accused Mrs Leigh Perrot of stealing a piece of white lace. When Mrs Leigh Perrot opened her parcel two lengths of lace, one black and one white, were disclosed. Remarking that the white lace must have been put in the parcel by mistake, Mrs Leigh Perrot returned it and left with her husband, only to be stopped at the corner of Abbey Churchyard by the male assistant from Smith's who demanded her name and address, which she willingly gave.

Miss Gregory and this assistant subsequently went to the Guildhall and placed a charge against Mrs Leigh Perrot of larceny. It was later supposed that the whole affair had been intended as a plot to force the wealthy Mr Leigh Perrot to part with a large sum of money in order to have the charge withdrawn. On 14 August, Mrs Leigh Perrot was committed to Ilchester Gaol, there to await trial at the next assizes. These were due to be held at Taunton in March, 1800. At this time such an offence was punishable by 14 years' transportation. Mr Leigh Perrot, who was then 65, and his wife nine years younger, declared that in the event of an adverse verdict he was prepared to sell his property in England and accompany his wife to her place of transportation. Meanwhile he declined to leave her and, having engaged Counsel for his wife's defence and selected witnesses to her perfect sanity and unblemished character, he accompanied her to Ilchester to be with her during the long months of waiting for the March assizes, her application for bail having been refused. Luckily they were not in the prison itself but were lodged in the house of the gaoler, one Edward Scadding. He appears to have been a humane and accommodating man and no limit seems to have been placed on their receiving visitors, letters, parcels and so on.

Some time before 11 January, 1800 Mrs Austen offered to send either Cassandra or Jane, or both of them, to be company for her sister-in-law for the rest of her imprisonment – a truly remarkable offer. We learn of this only indirectly from a letter to Mrs Leigh Perrot from her cousin, Sir Mountague Cholmeley. Mrs Leigh Perrot declined this kind offer saying that she could not let 'those Elegant young Women be ... Inmates in a Prison' and they could not be accommodated in the gaoler's house.[8]

The case was tried on 29 March 1800 in the Old Castle Hall, Taunton, which was packed for the occasion, and of which a full account was given in the weekly *Bath Chronicle* at the time. There were no Austens present, for Mrs Austen was unwell and Jane's brother James, 'a perfect Son' to Mrs Leigh Perrot, had broken his leg. A further offer of the company of Jane and Cassandra was rejected by Mrs Leigh Perrot, for as she said: 'to have two Young Creatures gazed at in a public Court would cut one to the very heart'.[9] The trial lasted nearly six hours but after retiring for less than 15 minutes the jury returned a verdict of 'not guilty'. The reporter of the *Star* for 31 March declared the scene in court after the acquittal to be 'extremely affecting' and one can guess the tremendous relief that the news must have been for the Leigh Perrots and all concerned for them.

An interesting point emerges from the reporting of this trial. The *Bath Chronicle* of 24 April 1800 contains the following:

'Mrs Leigh Perrott. This day is published, price Eighteen-pence, with Marginal Notes, The Trial of Mrs Leigh Perrott, by Wm. Legge. Esqr., of the Temple. Sold by Crosby, Stationer's Court, Pater-noster Row, London; and Mr Cruttwell, Bath.'

Knowing that Jane Austen must certainly have read this pamphlet of 'The Trial', one is tempted to speculate as to whether the Mr Cruttwell mentioned in the advertisement acted as Mr Crosby's agent in Bath, for he appears to have been a printer there, though he also sold patent medicines as a sideline. It would explain why Lord Brabourne said that Jane sold a novel (then called 'Susan' but published after her death as *Northanger Abbey*) to a Bath bookseller.[10] We know that in April 1809 Jane Austen, using an assumed name, attempted to persuade Mr Crosby to publish this same novel which he had purchased from her for £10 in 1803, but he refused to do so. In the end, it was her brother Henry who ultimately succeeded in re-purchasing the novel for her in 1816.

After this extraordinary incident the Leigh Perrots returned directly to Bath and resumed their old life there, though one might have thought that they had had enough of that city; 'Infernal Bath', as Sir Mountague Cholmeley called it, and which he was more convinced than ever was 'a Den of Villains, and a Harbour for all sort of Swindlers'.[11] More than this, the Leigh Perrots encouraged the Austens to settle in Bath the following year when Mr Austen retired.

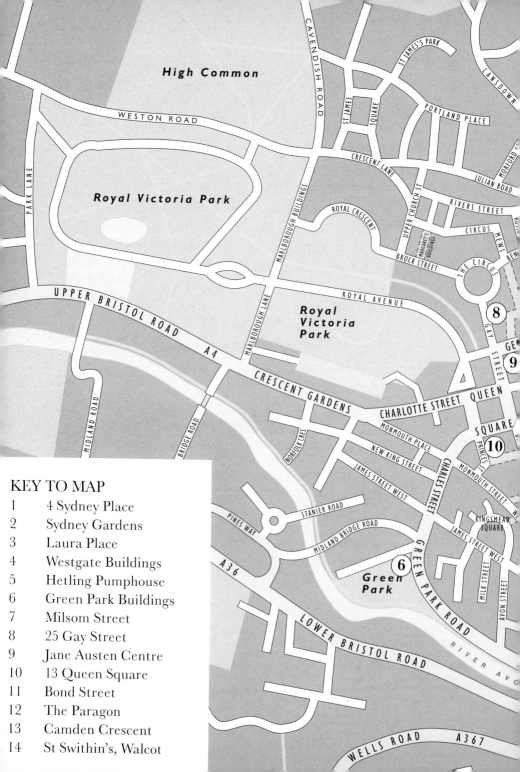

KEY TO MAP

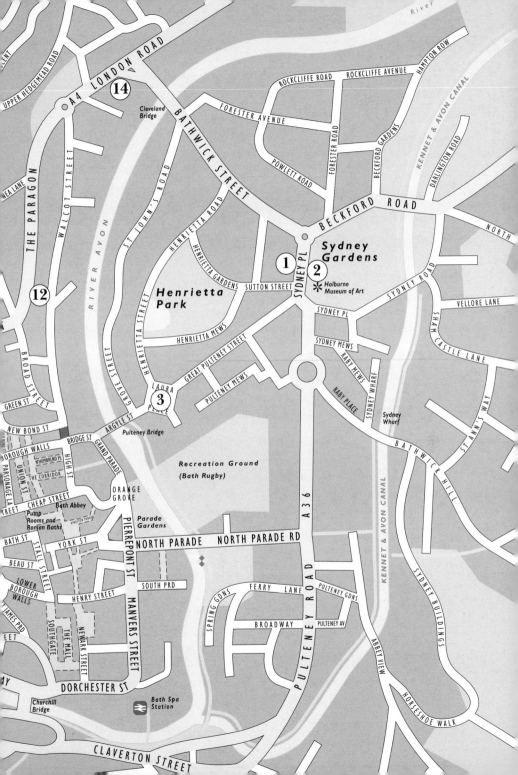

IV

Towards the end of the year 1800 the Reverend George Austen, at the age of seventy, decided to give up the living of Steventon and retire to Bath with his wife and daughters. He was succeeded as Rector by his son James.

This decision to settle in Bath came as a considerable shock to Jane, who had lived the first twenty-five years of her life at Steventon and was deeply attached to her home and the countryside there. In fact, family tradition has it that on first hearing the news she fainted away; certainly there is no doubt that for a time she was very unhappy. There is a gap of some weeks in her letters to Cassandra, who probably destroyed anything written by Jane at this time which might have expressed too intimately her feelings on the matter. However, by 3 January 1801 she could write to Cassandra: 'I get more & more reconciled to the idea of our removal. We have lived long enough in this Neighbourhood, the Basingstoke Balls are certainly on the decline, there is something interesting in the bustle of going away, & the prospect of spending future summers by the Sea or in Wales is very delightful'.

Luckily for posterity Cassandra remained at Godmersham until mid-February 1801 and Jane's letters during those weeks give the details of the upheaval at Steventon occasioned by the coming move to Bath. There was the dismissal and placing of the servants, the valuation and sale of livestock and furniture, the planning of the domestic arrangements, and above all, the choice of the new home in Bath. Jane and her mother were hoping to keep three servants and in the letter of 3 January 1801, she says, teasingly, to Cassandra: 'We plan having a steady Cook, & a young giddy Housemaid, with a sedate, middle aged Man, who is to undertake the double office of Husband to the former & sweetheart to the latter.– No Children of course to be allowed on either side'. All the best beds were to go with them, but they gradually rejected the idea of taking even a few favourite pieces of furniture; for as Jane continues: 'the trouble & risk of the removal would be more than the advantage of having them at a place, where everything may be purchased'. The various discussions about expenses were very relevant, as the family's future income would not be large. This letter from Jane ends with her saying: 'My father is doing all in his power to encrease his Income by raising his Tythes &c, & I do not despair of getting very nearly six hundred a year'.

The ideas as to exactly where the new home was to be varied from month to month, each of the Austens having a preference. They all knew Bath well and none of them wanted to live in Axford Buildings (nearby the Paragon), as Mrs Leigh Perrot would have liked; for as Jane writes (in the 3 January 1801 letter): 'we all unite in particular dislike of that part of the Town.' But, she says: 'There are three parts of Bath which we have thought of as likely to have Houses in them.—Westgate Buildings, Charles Street, & some of the short streets leading from Laura Place or Pulteney St'. Jane says that Westgate Buildings: 'tho' quite in the lower part of the Town are not badly situated themselves'. Mrs Austen asked Jane to tell Cassandra that she would 'do everything in her power to avoid Trim St' which Cassandra was thought to dislike. This was one of the first streets to be built outside the old City walls and although very fashionable when General Wolfe lived there, was no longer so by the end of the eighteenth century. Jane herself favoured Charles Street, which leads down from Queen Square to Green Park Buildings close by the river, where 'the Buildings are new', and its 'nearness to Kingsmead fields would be a pleasant circumstance'.[12] These fields have long since disappeared but anyone knowing Sheridan's play *The Rivals*, written in 1775, will remember that the final scene is set in these same Kingsmead Fields.

Their father wished to be across the river in 'the Environs of Laura-place', so Jane told Cassandra in her letter of 14 January 1801. Jane and her sister both liked this idea, though Jane feared that the streets near Laura Place would be above their price. Writing on 21 January she says: 'I join with you in wishing for the Environs of Laura place, but do not venture to expect it.—My Mother hankers after the Square [Queen Square] dreadfully'. Nevertheless, it seemed fairly certain that the Austens' new home would be somewhere on the new Bathwick estate, across the river.

There followed next the actual house-hunting. Mrs Austen and her daughters had an invitation from the Leigh Perrots to stay at the Paragon whilst they looked round for a suitable house. Various farewell visits were paid and in early May the Steventon party broke up. It was finally decided that Jane and her mother should travel on ahead to Bath, in spite of the fact that Jane had felt her sister's presence there as well to be an indispensable necessity. Cassandra and her father had other separate visits to make and they were expected to join the others at Bath some weeks later. One result of this arrangement was that there are three interesting letters from Jane to her sister telling of the progress of the search for the new home.

All three are from the Paragon; the first is dated Tuesday, 5 May 1801, and is written as Jane says: 'from my own room up two pair of stairs, with everything very comfortable about me'. She describes the successful journey there in 'charming weather', which their mother 'bore without any fatigue'. Then follows news of the progress of the house-hunting. It seems that her uncle and aunt had ideas of a house in Seymour Street for the Austens and they were also able to tell Jane that all the houses in New King Street were too small, confirming Jane's 'own idea of them'. The cheapness of food in Bath was to be one of its many advantages and Jane mentions the prices of various items, saying that she was 'not without hopes of tempting Mrs Lloyd to settle in Bath;—Meat is only 8d. per pound, butter 12d. and cheese $9^1/_2$d'. Bath possessed excellent markets—the one adjoining the Guildhall is still in existence. *The New Bath Guide, or Useful Pocket Companion* (printed by C. Pope) for 1764 says that the markets were 'supplied with the greatest Variety of all sorts of Provisions, and generally at very reasonable prices', and also that Bath excelled all other English inland towns for the 'Goodness and Quantity of the Sea Fish brought to it', besides freshwater fish 'daily taken in the River Avon'. Jane, however, thought the price of fish very dear and tells Cassandra so.

Jane added another page to this letter the same evening, telling how 'When my Uncle went to take his second glass of water, I walked with him, & in our morning's circuit we looked at two Houses in Green Park Buildings, one of which pleased me very well'. The dining-room was described as 'of a comfortable size', and the apartment over the Drawing-room pleased Jane particularly. The only doubt was 'about the Dampness of the Offices, of which there were symptoms'. Only the western side of Green Park Buildings remains today; the eastern side, destroyed in the bombing raids of 1942, has been replaced by blocks of council flats.

Jane added a final page to this letter on the Wednesday, giving Cassandra some news of the current fashions. She begins with a detailed account of the new dress being made for her in the latest style by a Mrs Mussell, then tells how she and her mother have both ordered new bonnets, though she finds her 'straw bonnet looking very much like other people's & quite as smart'. She also informs Cassandra that bonnets of cambric muslin 'are a good deal worn, & some of them are very pretty', and 'Black gauze Cloaks are worn as much as anything'. This last item completes the letter but the postscript is of interest as it says: 'Last night we walked by the Canal'. This is the Kennet and Avon Canal which is on the south side of the river in Bath and links the River Avon with the River Kennet in Berkshire, and along which goods used to be transported from the West Country to London and other parts. That part of the canal from Bath towards Bradford-on-Avon, to which Jane Austen is here referring, still provides, as it did in her day, very delightful walks along its banks.

Jane's next letter, of Tuesday 12 May 1801, gives more details of her activities in Bath. Her aunt had arranged several card parties for her guests. Jane was rather bored with these small gatherings, which she thought might be 'less intolerable' if they were larger. She had been to church twice on Sunday and 'after evening service walked a little in the Crescent fields'. She had been to the last ball of the season at the Upper Rooms but it was very sparsely attended; this was not surprising, as we are told in Jane's previous letter that 'Bath is getting so very empty'. Before tea the ball 'was rather a dull affair', and Jane says: 'Think of four couple, surrounded by about an hundred people, dancing in the upper rooms at Bath!' However after tea they 'cheered up' and 'tho' it was shockingly & inhumanly thin for this place, there were people enough I suppose to have made five or six very pretty Basingstoke assemblies'. She also notes that the recommended house in Seymour Street was 'not inviting;– the largest room downstairs, was not much more than fourteen feet square', so it was rejected.

A third and final letter to Cassandra of Thursday, 21 May 1801 shows that thus far the house-hunting had met with no success. Jane writes that their views on Green Park Buildings 'seem all at an end'. The dampness, 'with reports of discontented families & putrid fevers, has given the coup de grace.– We have now nothing in veiw'. She looks forward to Cassandra's joining them, all being well, on Monday 1 June.

Then follows an account of a long walk to Weston village with a friend, a Mrs Chamberlayne. Jane says: 'It would have amused you to see our progress;– we went up by Sion Hill, & returned across the fields;... we posted away under a fine hot sun,... stopping for nothing, & crossing the Church Yard at Weston with as much expedition as if we were afraid of being buried alive'.

This letter finishes with the following injunction to Cassandra: 'When you have made Martha's bonnet you must make her a cloak of the same sort of materials; they are very much worn here, in different forms'.

The Weston walk was followed by another with Mrs Chamberlayne, this time to Lyncombe and Widcombe, across the River Avon and a considerable distance from the Paragon. Jane says: 'Mrs Chamberlayne's pace was not quite so magnificent on this second trial as in the first; it was nothing more than I could keep up with, without effort; & for many, many Yards together on a raised narrow footpath I led the way.– The walk was very beautiful, as my companion agreed, whenever I made the observation'.

The arrival of Cassandra and her father in Bath was now imminent; in fact Jane had made an engagement for her sister for 4 June, when friends would take them to a display of fireworks in the Sydney Gardens. Opposite

The Assembly Rooms, front entrance

No. 4 Sydney Place

those delightful gardens was the house that the Austens finally chose for their new home but we shall never know exactly how that choice was arrived at, because with Cassandra's appearance in Bath the letters ceased.

We do know that the following advertisement appeared in the *Bath Chronicle* on Thursday, 21 May 1801:

> 'To be disposed of . The lease of No. 4, Sydney-Place, three years and a quarter of which are unexpired at Midsummer.—The situation is desirable, the Rent very low, and the Landlord is bound by covenant to paint the two first floors this summer.— A premium will therefore be expected. For particulars apply to Messrs. Watts and Forman, Cornwall-Buildings, Bath'.

Sydney Place is on Bathwick Estate across the river at the far end of Pulteney Street and overlooks the Sydney Gardens. Although today Bath extends a considerable distance around and beyond it, in Jane Austen's day Sydney Place had the great advantage of being on the edge of the open country. This would have given it a special appeal to the Austen family.

The four-storeyed terraced houses, facing east, are lofty and elegant though somewhat smaller than those in adjoining Pulteney Street. No. 4 is today divided into flats and a plaque on the house records the fact that Jane Austen once lived in it. It is a pleasant and easy walk from there into the town, for although Pulteney Street is lengthy (it is well over 300 yards long) its pavements are broad and spacious and, above all, completely flat; something to be welcomed in Bath where so many of the streets are steeply sloping. Immediately across Pulteney Bridge is the centre of the town with the markets, shops, Abbey, Pump Room, libraries, etc., all to hand. The inhabitants of the New Pulteney Estate, as it was sometimes called, also possessed their own chapel – Laura Chapel, another of Bath's proprietary chapels, opened in 1792 on the Pulteney Street side of Pulteney Bridge. This was probably the one to which Jane sometimes referred in letters as 'our chapel'.

In Jane Austen's day the Sydney Gardens were one of Bath's greatest outdoor attractions and they are frequently mentioned in her letters. We can learn more about them from an early 19th-century description: 'Sydney-

Gardens is one of the most prominent, pleasing, and elegant features attached to the City of Bath... Upon gala-nights, the music, singing, cascades, transparencies, fire-works, and superb illuminations, render these gardens very similar to Vauxhall... and music also enlivens the scene, when public breakfasts are given'.[13] The same writer calls the Labyrinth there an object of curiosity and goes on to say that 'The inns and outs necessary to be made, it is said, measure half a mile'. Jane herself had once teasingly written to Cassandra: 'It would be very pleasant to be near Sidney Gardens! we might go into the Labyrinth every day'.[14]

Although Brunel built his famous Great Western Railway through the Sydney Gardens in 1840, the elegant bridges spanning it and stone balustrades along its length are a positive attraction in what is still a very pleasant park.

Each summer during their years of residence in Bath was enlivened by a visit to the seaside. First Sidmouth in 1801, then Dawlish in 1802, followed by Ramsgate in 1803, where Jane first met Mary Gibson, Frank Austen's bride-to-be, whom she and Cassandra liked immensely. Later in 1803 and again in 1804 they went to Lyme Regis, which Jane thought a delightful place. She was to use it later as the seaside town in *Persuasion*, in which she wrote: 'a very strange stranger it must be, who does not see charms in the immediate environs of Lyme, to make him wish to know it better'.[15]

During one of these summer holidays, Jane is supposed to have met the young man whom she might one day have married. Tragically he died quite suddenly very soon afterwards. Our best account of this comes from Mrs Louisa Bellas, daughter of Jane Austen's niece, Anna Lefroy.[16] It was also during these years that Jane, while on a visit to her friends the Biggs, at Manydown Park in Hampshire in December 1802, received a sudden proposal of marriage from their brother, Harris Bigg-Wither. This she at first accepted and then next morning rejected as she realised that she could not marry someone whom she liked but did not love. Extremely upset by the incident, she insisted on returning to Bath immediately. These events may help to explain why no letters from Jane to Cassandra for the three years at Sydney Place survive. It is improbable that the sisters were never parted all that time and that no letters were written, although certainly at such a period in Jane's life Cassandra would have wanted to be with her as much as possible. The distress occasioned by these incidents may also be one reason why Jane did so little writing during the years in Bath, although she did revise and complete *Northanger Abbey* and is also thought to have written the fragment *The Watsons*.

In addition to these two events of a very personal nature in Jane Austen's life, there was the fact that Mr Austen, now over 70, was in poor health during these last years before his death in 1805 and no doubt Cassandra and Jane had much more to do at home during this time. We learn something of this in a later letter from Jane to her brother Francis, describing Mr Austen's last illness and saying that it began with 'a return of the feverish complaint, which he had been subject to for the last three years'. Mrs Austen also was very ill during their residence at 4 Sydney Place and although she recovered completely, to live another 20 years, her illness must have given her family a great deal of anxiety. She was nursed by Cassandra and Jane and had an excellent doctor, a Mr Bowen. The whole episode was commemorated in the following lines by Mrs Austen herself, entitled 'Dialogue between Death and Mrs A':

Says Death 'I've been trying these three weeks or more
To seize on Old Madam here at number four,
Yet I still try in vain, tho' she's turn'd of threescore,
To what is my ill success oweing'?
I'll tell you, old Fellow, if you cannot guess,
To what you're indebted for your ill success;
To the Prayers of my Husband, whose love I possess,
To the care of my Daughters, whom Heaven will bless;
To the skill and attention of BOWEN. [17]

It is obvious that life in Sydney Place, Bath, was a totally different sort of existence from the one which Jane had enjoyed at Steventon, in the quiet Hampshire countryside. There was so much more going on all the time, there were so many more shops and so much more shopping to be undertaken, so many more calls to receive and to pay, so many libraries and so much more entertainment, of which to take advantage. With all this in addition to the more personal reasons, it is no wonder that Jane wrote little whilst living in Bath.

V

During these years in Sydney Place Jane Austen may not have written a great deal but without doubt she experienced much, something which is apparent in her later works especially perhaps in *Persuasion,* her last novel and one with a sad and autumnal quality about it. For many this is her finest work and it is certainly the most loving and beautiful. It was published, together with *Northanger Abbey* a few months after Jane's death, but thirteen years separated the two works.[18]

These two novels have in common the fact that they are both set for a great part of the time against the background of a real place, namely Bath, whereas Jane Austen usually placed her characters in imaginary towns and villages. Although never attempting a direct description of the city or trying to view it as a whole, Jane nevertheless was able, out of her own experience, so faithfully to portray Bath scenes and society that they come alive with vivid intensity for those of us reading these two novels today. So realistic are the descriptions of Bath that it is almost impossible to look at the city from Beechen Cliff and not think of Catherine Morland and the Tilneys there; nor to walk up Belmont to Camden Crescent and not think of Anne Elliot walking there with Captain Wentworth; or to be in Milsom Street and not think of Admiral Croft gazing at the picture of a ship in a shop window, so unlike any other ship he ever saw.

Written when Jane was in her early twenties, *Northanger Abbey* is set in the final years of the 18th-century. It is not perhaps one of the great novels but with its prevailing mood of lightness and gaiety it is perfect of its kind and tells what happened to its lovable and youthful heroine, Catherine Morland, when taken by her friends, the Allens, to undergo 'all the difficulties and dangers of a six weeks' residence in Bath'.[19]

In the early part of the book we learn that the visitors entered the city by crossing the Avon at the Old Bridge[20] and were driven up Stall Street to their hotel, probably the White Hart, opposite the Abbey Churchyard. Here they stayed for a day or two before going into lodgings in Pulteney Street, which had then only recently been built.

The Lower and Upper Rooms and the Pump Room, which Jane herself knew so well, all appear in turn in the pages of *Northanger Abbey*. Knowing no one in Bath, the Allens took the first opportunity of visiting the Upper Rooms with Catherine, where unfortunately they were ignored by everyone present. The same happened at first when they went to the Pump Room, at mid-day the centre of attraction for all able-bodied and fashionable visitors. Here the Allens and Catherine 'paraded up and down for an hour, looking at every body and speaking to no one'.[21]

It was when they went to the Lower Rooms that their luck changed, for here the Master of Ceremonies introduced Henry Tilney to Catherine as her partner. Henry was a charming young man of about twenty-five and a country clergyman in Gloucestershire, the younger son of General Tilney of Northanger Abbey; so Catherine 'felt herself in high luck'. Henry teasingly asked her what she had been doing in Bath so far and learned that she had already been to a ball, a theatre, and a concert, and that she was very much pleased with everything, particularly the shops, for 'one can step out of doors and get a thing in five minutes', whereas at home the nearest shops were eight miles away.[22]

Mrs Allen's ceaseless wish to meet some acquaintance whilst in Bath was finally granted when she met an old schoolfellow, a Mrs Thorpe, at the Pump Room. The two young Thorpes became friendly with Catherine and it was with Isabella Thorpe that Catherine made her famous dash through the centre of Bath in pursuit of two young men whom Isabella had observed staring at them in the Pump Room. The girls set off from Abbey Churchyard through the archway, across Cheap Street and up Union Passage. At that time this would have been the regular way to reach Milsom Street from the Pump Room, Union Street not being in existence until 1806. In the same year New Bond Street, until then only a foot passage, was opened as a carriageway. There are quite a number of these passages in Bath, which still make pleasant places to shop or walk in without

Bath Abbey, West Front, and Abbey Churchyard

The Circus, looking down Gay Street to Beechen Cliff

hindrance from traffic. Finally, in Milsom Street, the girls overtook and passed the two offending young men without incident, except that Isabella 'was so far from seeking to attract their notice, that she looked back at them only three times'.[23] From Milsom Street it was only a short distance to Edgar Buildings, forming the north side of George Street, where the Thorpes were staying.

Later Jane describes what she herself knew so well, the visitors' Sunday routine of walking in the Royal Crescent or Crescent Fields after church. Catherine was in the Royal Crescent on the Sunday when John Thorpe proposed a drive to Clifton for the following day. She was to have gone then for a walk with Henry Tilney and his sister, so, shaking off her companions, Catherine hastened from the Crescent to confirm this. The Tilneys were returning to their lodgings in Milsom Street, felt no doubt by Jane to be a suitable place for the wealthy General Tilney's family to stay. Catherine almost ran along Brock Street, through the Circus, Gay Street and George Street, and managed to catch the Tilneys just as they reached their door. Once again one is a little surprised to learn what determined walkers Jane Austen's heroines usually were. Catherine ultimately succeeded in having her outing with Henry and Eleanor Tilney and this was the celebrated occasion when the three young people made the steep climb up to Beechen Cliff, already mentioned as giving such wonderful views over Bath. Catherine found the whole occasion quite delightful.

The rest of the book deals with the deepening love of Catherine and Henry, first in Bath and then at Northanger Abbey, finishing with their becoming engaged at Catherine's home in Wiltshire; a happy ending entirely in keeping with the spirit of this novel.

In *Persuasion* we find ourselves once more in Bath, but Bath with a difference; its attraction as a fashionable centre had begun to wane and its whole atmosphere to change and to mellow. The period is nearly twenty years after that of *Northanger Abbey* and the chief characters, too, are older, about ten years older than Catherine Morland and her friends. Jane has written here what is above all else a love story, set against the background of the years of the Napoleonic Wars, but at a time when many naval officers, retired or on half pay following one of the periods of peace during that conflict, settled themselves in Bath. The story tells how the hero and heroine, Captain Frederick Wentworth and Anne Elliot, are brought together once more, when they encounter each other again seven years after Anne had been persuaded by her family to refuse Captain Wentworth's hand.

When Anne's father, the arrogant and conceited Sir Walter Elliot, decided for reasons of economy to let his country house and move into town, Bath was felt to be the only alternative to London possible for a man of his rank: 'he might there be important at comparatively little expense'.[24] Knowing Bath so well, Jane was able in *Persuasion* to place her characters in those parts of the city suitable to their income and to their station in life. Thus we find Sir Walter Elliot, with his daughter Elizabeth, in a furnished house in the then comparatively new Camden Place (now Camden Crescent) overlooking the city, 'a lofty, dignified situation, such as becomes a man of consequence'.[25] Here later Anne joined them. The Elliots were near enough to Lansdown Crescent for Sir Walter's heir, Mr William Elliot, after dining there, to pay an evening call upon his relations. Lady Russell, a widow of quiet tastes and 'extremely well provided for',[26] was in lodgings in Rivers Street, only a short distance from Camden Place. Lady Dalrymple and her daughters, those highborn relations of Sir Walter's of whom he made such a fuss, were in the more exclusive new Bathwick Estate across the river, where they had 'taken a house, for three months, in Laura-place, and would be living in style'.[27]

Colonel Wallis, 'a highly respectable man, perfectly the gentleman'[28] and with whom Sir Walter had condescended to appear arm in arm in the streets of Bath, was in a furnished house in Marlborough Buildings. Completed in 1791, these were described in the *New Bath Guide, or Useful Pocket Companion* (printed by R.Cruttwell) for 1799 as an 'elegant row of houses' 'just finished to the west of the Royal Crescent'.

Anne Elliot's old schoolfellow, Mrs Smith, now a poor widow crippled with arthritis, was in far humbler lodgings. These were in Westgate Buildings, where Anne visited her, much to Sir Walter's disgust. 'Westgate-buildings!' said he; 'and who is Miss Anne Elliot to be visiting in Westgate-buildings?'[29] However the close proximity of the Hot Bath must have been very convenient for such a helpless invalid.

When Admiral Croft, who had rented Sir Walter's Somersetshire home, Kellynch Hall, came to Bath with his wife to take the waters, they had lodgings in Gay Street. Sir Walter, after enquiries as to the whereabouts of his tenant, felt that his carriage could stop at the door of a house in Gay Street but did not consider the Crofts of sufficient social consequence to be introduced to the Dalrymples in Laura Place. As his eldest daughter Elizabeth said: 'We had better leave the Crofts to find their own level. There are several odd-looking men walking about here, who, I am told, are sailors. The Crofts will associate with them !' What Sir Walter and Miss Elliot did not appreciate was that the Admiral and his wife had no interest in or reverence for Sir Walter and 'considered their intercourse with the Elliots as a mere matter of form, and not in the least likely to afford them any pleasure'.[30]

We learn much of naval officers and the Navy in *Persuasion* and Jane's own deep affection for both, inspired no doubt by her own two sailor brothers, is very apparent. Anne loved to watch the Crofts, who were always together, and 'to see the Admiral's hearty shake of the hand when he encountered an old friend, and observe their eagerness of conversation when occasionally forming into a little knot of the navy, Mrs Croft looking as intelligent and keen as any of the officers around her'.[31]

Then there is the charming picture we get of the Admiral's astonishment on seeing a painting of a ship in a shop window in Milsom Street and exclaiming to Anne in his bluff and cheerful way: 'What queer fellows your fine painters must be, to think that anybody would venture their lives in such a shapeless old cockleshell... I wonder where that boat was built!' (laughing heartily) — 'I would not venture over a horsepond in it'.[32]

For Sir Walter Elliot the 'worst of Bath was, the number of its plain women'. We hear that he once stood in a shop in Bond Street and 'counted eighty-seven women go by, one after another, without there being a tolerable face among them'.[33]

The characters in *Persuasion* move between Bath and the country, at Uppercross or Kellynch, and pay a visit to Jane Austen's beloved Lyme. Anne, like Jane herself, infinitely preferred country life to that of the town. The 'dash of other carriages, the heavy rumble of carts and drays, the bawling of newsmen, muffin-men and milk-men, and the ceaseless clink of pattens' were some of the sounds which greeted the ears of Lady Russell and Anne as they crossed the Old Bridge and drove through streets 'smoking in rain' upwards to Camden Place. Anne hated this tumult and noise for she disliked Bath but Lady Russell felt that they 'belonged to the winter pleasures' and 'her spirits rose under their influence'.[34]

Many visitors still came to Bath but were apt to shun the public balls and assemblies and to despise the mixed crowds now found there. The fashion of holding private parties had spread amongst the more select visitors. The Elliots never attended or gave anything else. They made an exception for concerts and because of this we have the famous scene in the Octagon Room at the Upper Rooms, where Anne and Captain Wentworth enjoyed such a promising conversation. Apart from this concert and one mention of the theatre there are scarcely any allusions in *Persuasion* to public entertainments and not a word about dances in any of the Rooms. Not that Anne at twenty-seven was too old (Jane herself danced at Southampton when over thirty); it was just that Bath's whole atmosphere had changed. Instead of the Pump Room or Crescent, people frequently met at such places as Molland's, the pastry cook's shop in Milsom Street. Here Anne encountered Captain Wentworth for the first time after his return from Lyme, when he, unknown to her, had come to Bath once more to solicit her hand. She was sheltering from the rain when he entered the shop with a party of friends. Although she had the advantage of seeing him first and being a little more prepared, her feelings nevertheless were excruciating, 'agitation, pain, pleasure, a something between delight and misery'.[35]

From this time on the story proceeds fairly quickly to its inevitable conclusion. We have Anne's famous drive with Lady Russell down Pulteney Street, when espying Captain Wentworth and seeing Lady Russell's fixed gaze out of the carriage window, Anne wondered what Lady Russell's opinion of Captain Wentworth at this stage would be. To her complete astonishment Lady Russell comments only on some curtains at one of the windows; she had not noticed Captain Wentworth at all!

Soon afterwards, the Musgrove family party arrived in Bath and stayed at the White Hart, Bath's principal family hotel, opposite the Pump Room in Abbey Churchyard. It was here, in the family's private sitting-room, that Captain Wentworth wrote a letter to Anne declaring his unchanged love for her. It was a situation of extreme poignancy, for as he wrote he could overhear Anne, in another corner of the room, making her own wonderful declaration to Captain Harville of the constancy of woman's love.

At this time came the discovery of Mrs Clay's connivance with Mr Elliot, when she was noticed from the White Hart windows deep in conversation with Mr Elliot under the colonnade, after they had been seen turning the corner of Bath Street together.

The final scene of *Persuasion* takes place in Union Street, just below Milsom Street. (We can see from this how Jane Austen had kept in touch with Bath, for Union Street was not opened until after she had left the city.) From here the lovers slowly 'paced the gradual ascent' to Camden Place, heedless of all else and all others and 'more exquisitely happy, perhaps, in their re-union, than when it had been first projected'.[36]

VI

The summer of 1804 saw the end of the Austens' lease of No. 4 Sydney Place and it was not renewed. Certainly by the September, when the family were at Lyme, the house already had other occupants. Writing from there to Cassandra, who had gone to Weymouth, Jane says on 14 September 1804: 'The Coles have got their infamous plate upon our door.– I dare say *that* makes a great part of the massy plate so much talked of'.

When the Austens returned to Bath in October 1804 it was to a house – No. 3 – in those Green Park Buildings which in 1801 they had rejected as unhealthy. They appear to have taken out a six months' lease.

In December of that same year there occurred the death of Mrs Lefroy, wife of their near neighbour the Reverend George Lefroy of Ashe, following a fall from her horse; a sad blow for them all and particularly for Jane, whose dear friend she was.

Then, on 21 January 1805, Jane wrote from Green Park Buildings to her brother Frank to tell him the sad news of their father's death. There are actually two letters, both saying much the same, as she wrote again on 22 January when she realised that by then Frank would have reached Portsmouth. Mr Austen was ill for only forty-eight hours before he died, 'a death almost as free from suffering as his Children could have wished', from a return of the same 'feverish complaint' which he had often suffered during the previous three years. Speaking of their sad loss Jane says: 'His tenderness as a Father, who can do justice to?' She finished by telling Frank that James was expected next day and that the funeral was to be on Saturday (i.e. 26 January) at Walcot church; also, that in spite of offers of hospitality from Steventon, Jane thought that they would remain on in Bath: 'We must have this house for three months longer, & here we shall probably stay till the end of that time'.

James and Henry were at Mr Austen's funeral and the three older sons

No. 4 Sydney Place, interior

No. 25 Gay Street

together made provision for their mother and two sisters (Charles at twenty-five and still a Commander was not expected to contribute) to produce an income for them of at least £450 per annum. This did not compare badly with the £600 per annum which, in 1801, Jane had hoped for her father. As Henry Austen said: 'I really think that My Mother & sisters will be to the full as rich as ever. They will not only suffer no personal deprivation, but will be able to pay occasional visits of health and pleasure to their friends'. Mrs Austen wrote some years later to Mrs Leigh Perrot that £122 per annum 'is the whole of my own property, my good children having supplied all the rest'.[37]

In the April following Mr Austen's death Cassandra was away at Ibthorp with their great friend Martha Lloyd, whose mother was ill and died towards the end of the visit. Martha was then asked to come and live with Mrs Austen and her two daughters, an arrangement which Jane referred to as their partnership with Martha.

The family had left Green Park Buildings on Lady Day, 1805, and thereafter were installed in lodgings at 25 Gay Street, from which Jane's two letters to Cassandra at Ibthorp were written. Gay Street, as previously mentioned, was built by John Wood the elder to connect his Queen Square with the Circus. The Street slopes fairly steeply and No. 25 is about halfway up on the east side. The houses are elegant and smaller than those of the Circus and the Square. Nowadays a large number of them are let out as offices and No. 25 at present houses a firm of dental surgeons. Its outward appearance, however, is unchanged and its position in the town as convenient today as the Austens must have found it in 1805. Mrs Austen had always liked Gay Street and, when house-hunting four years earlier, had had her eye on a house at the bottom end of it. No doubt after the loss of her husband she was glad to be that much nearer to her brother in the Paragon, who, at this time, had shown her 'every imaginable kindness'. She was, in these new lodgings, separated from him only by the length of George Street.

Jane's first letter to Cassandra from No. 25 is dated Monday, 8 April 1805. Mentioning the really wonderful weather Jane says: 'We do nothing but walk about'. On Sunday morning they had walked in the Royal Crescent but had found it too hot and had retreated to the Crescent Fields. On leaving chapel that afternoon they had walked up to Lansdown Crescent for tea at No. 19. On Monday morning they had been 'to see Miss Chamberlayne look hot on horseback' – and Jane adds: 'Seven years & four months ago we went to the same Riding-house to see Miss Lefroy's performance!—What a different set are we now moving in! But seven years I suppose are enough to change every pore of one's skin & every feeling of one's mind'. Jane was thirty by now and obviously felt that her experiences over the previous seven years had qualified her to write thus.

Bath possessed two riding schools at this time, Ryle's in Monmouth Street and Mr Dash's in Montpelier Row. Jane and her mother probably visited the latter. There, the *New Bath Guide, or Useful Pocket Companion* for 1799 says, 'Ladies and Gentlemen amuse themselves every morning, and are instructed in the art of horsemanship', gratis if they kept their horse on the premises, otherwise 5/3d. a single lesson. Adjoining the Riding School was 'an elegant and commodious Tennis-Court', opened in 1777.

In addition to enjoying the lovely spring weather Jane and her widowed mother were invited out to a number of tea parties, and Jane says: 'We have therefore offered ourselves & our quietness', and she adds that because of this they feel that their own 'Tea & Sugar will last a great while'.

The other letter that Jane wrote to Cassandra from Gay Street is dated Sunday evening, 21 April 1805. Jane had been to a concert and, in view of her mourning, had had crape sleeves added to her dress for the occasion. She says also: 'on my head I wore my crape & flowers, but I do not think it looked particularly well'. She had been invited to a 'Grand Sydney-Garden Breakfast' by Mrs Leigh Perrot, but had declined. Jane had never been over fond of this aunt and one can see this in a much later letter to Cassandra (from Southampton, 20 November 1808) when, remarking on a very complaining letter that their mother had received from Mrs Leigh Perrot, Jane says: 'the discontentedness of it shocked & surprised her— but *I* see nothing in it out of Nature—tho' a sad nature'.

Jane had accompanied her cousins, George and Mary Cooke, who were in rooms in Alfred Place, and three other young people to the Sydney

Gardens for an afternoon. George, the younger son of Cassandra, wife of the Reverend Samuel Cooke and Mrs Austen's cousin, was about twenty-five at this time. Jane was always very fond of him.

This last letter that Jane wrote from Bath ends with her saying that the Leigh Perrots had drunk tea with them the evening before, and she had felt obliged to invite them again for the next evening 'to avoid anything that might seem a slight to them'.

There are no further letters from Bath. As usual the Austens left the city during the summer months, but in the *Memoir* written by her nephew, Mr J.E. Austen Leigh, we are told that they returned to Bath that winter and were in lodgings in Trim Street, from where Mrs Austen wrote a letter to her daughter-in-law, Mrs James Austen, on 10 April 1806.[38]

But already they were thinking of moving on and in the summer of 1806 Mrs Austen, with her daughters and Martha Lloyd, departed for Clifton and thence, towards the autumn, to Southampton. So far as we know Jane never came to Bath again but through her relations, the Leigh Perrots, who moved from the Paragon to No. 49 Pulteney Street in 1811, and through Lady Bridges and her daughters, she always kept in touch with what went on there.

From Southampton Jane wrote to Cassandra on 1 July 1808: 'It will be two years tomorrow since we left Bath for Clifton, with what happy feelings of Escape!' Jane is thought to have revised *Northanger Abbey* whilst at Bath and perhaps she herself was speaking when Isabella Thorpe says to Catherine Morland: 'I get so immoderately sick of Bath; your brother and I were agreeing this morning that, though it is vastly well to be here for a few weeks, we would not live here for millions'.[39] The Austens really were – what Isabella only pretended to be – country lovers born and bred. They were not averse to Society but preferred the neighbourliness of village life and occasional visits to country houses and parsonages to living in a city. Even Southampton was not ideal for them and in 1809 they joyfully moved to the cottage on Edward Austen's estate in the little Hampshire village of Chawton, which was Jane's beloved home for the rest of her life.

Notes

In these Notes, the following abbreviations apply:

Austen Papers: *Austen Papers 1704-1856* ed. R.A.Austen-Leigh. London: Spottiswoode, Ballantyne & Co. 1942

Egan: *Walks Through Bath* by P.Egan. Bath: Meyler and Son, 1819.

Letters:*Jane Austen's Letters*, ed. Deirdre Le Faye. Oxford: Oxford University Press, 1995.

NA: *Northanger Abbey* by Jane Austen.

P: *Persuasion* by Jane Austen.

1. see *The Building of Bath* by Bryan Little (London: Collins 1947), p. 99.
2. Egan, p.59.
3. Egan, p.69.
4. Letters, 2 June 1799; 11 June 1799.
5. Letters, 30 November 1800.
6. NA Ch. 14.
7. P Ch. 23.
8. Austen Papers, p.198.
9. Austen Papers, p.206.
10. *Letters of Jane Austen*, ed. Lord Brabourne, 2 Vols (London: R Bentley, 1884) Vol I, p. 76.
11. Austen Papers, p.202.
12. Letters, 3 January 1801.
13. Egan, p.182.
14. Letters, 21 January 1801. Jane spelled Sydney with an 'i'.
15. P Ch. 11.
16. *Jane Austen A Survey* by C. Linklater Thomson (London: H. Marshall, 1929), p.201.
17. *Collected Poems and Verse of the Austen Family* ed. David Selwyn (Jane Austen Society/Carcanet Press 1996), p.30.
18. NA, originally called 'Susan' was written 1798-99 and revised in 1803.
19. NA Ch. 2.
20. Replaced in 1966 by the new Churchill Bridge.
21. NA Ch. 3.
22. NA Ch. 3.
23. NA Ch. 7.
24. P Ch. 2.
25. P Ch. 15.
26. P Ch. 1.

27. P Ch. 16.
28. P Ch. 15.
29. P Ch. 17.
30. P Ch. 18.
31. P Ch. 18.
32. P Ch. 18.
33. P Ch. 15.
34. P Ch. 14.
35. P Ch. 19.
36. P Ch. 23.
37. Austen Papers, pp.235 and 264
38. Austen Papers, p. 237.
39. NA Ch. 10.

Index

Illustrations are on pages numbered in bold type